EYE ON THE SKY

WHEN TORNADOES TOUCH DOWN

Gareth Stevens PUBLISHING

BY THERESE SHEA

Please visit our website, www.garethstevens.com. For a free color catalog of all our high-quality books, call toll free 1-800-542-2595 or fax 1-877-542-2596.

Cataloging-in-Publication Data

Shea, Therese.
When tornadoes touch down / by Therese Shea.
p. cm. — (Eye on the sky)
Includes index.
ISBN 978-1-4824-2896-4 (pbk.)
ISBN 978-1-4824-2897-1 (6 pack)
ISBN 978-1-4824-2898-8 (library binding)
1. Tornadoes — Juvenile literature. I. Shea, Therese. II. Title.
QC955.2 S54 2016
551.55'3—d23

Published in 2016 by
Gareth Stevens Publishing
111 East 14th Street, Suite 349
New York, NY 10003

Designer: Laura Bowen
Editor: Kristen Rajczak

Photo credits: Cover, p. 1 Cultura Science/Jason Persoff Stormdoctor/Oxford Scientific/Getty Images; cover, pp. 1–32 (series art) Nik Merkulov/Shutterstock.com; p. 4 Gunter Nezhoda/Shutterstock.com; p. 5 Willoughby Owen/Moment/Getty Images; pp. 7, 9 Minerva Studio/Shutterstock.com; p. 8 (all) Vanessa Ezekowitz/Wikimedia Commons; p. 11 (top) Vizual Studios/Shutterstock.com; p. 11 (middle) Benjamin Simeneta/Shutterstock.com; p. 11 (bottom) Melissa Brandes/Shutterstock.com; pp. 12, 27 (NSSL car), 29 (right) Carsten Peter/National Geographic/Getty Images; p. 13 Cheryl E. Davis/ Shutterstock.com; p. 14 (left) James E. Knopf/Shutterstock.com; p. 14 (right) Ken Shulze/Shutterstock.com; p. 15 Dustie/Shutterstock.com; p. 16 (sign) Sari ONeal/Shutterstock.com; p. 16 (shelter) Richard A McMillan/ Shutterstock.com; pp. 17, 24 (all) AFP/Getty Images; p. 18 Larry Miller/Science Source/Getty Images; p. 19 Jim Reed/Science Source/Getty Images; p. 20 lafoto/Shutterstock.com; p. 21 Miami Herald/INACTIVE/ Hulton Archive/Getty Images; p. 22 Joe Raedle/Getty Images News/Getty Images; p. 23 Benjamin Krain/ Getty Images News/Getty Images; p. 25 (main) Topical Press Agency/Hulton Archive/Getty Images; p. 25 (inset) New York Public Library/Science Source/Getty Images; p. 27 (meteorologists) Kim Steele/ Photodisc/Getty Images; p. 29 (left) Mike Theiss/National Geographic/Getty Images.

Printed in the United States of America

CPSIA compliance information: Batch #CS15GS: For further information contact Gareth Stevens, New York, New York at 1-800-542-2595.

CONTENTS

Words in the glossary appear in **bold** type the first time they are used in the text.

TORNADO ALERT!

Imagine you're at home doing homework one afternoon. You're playing music softly. Suddenly, you're startled by a long, high-pitched alarm. You quickly realize it's your town's tornado-warning siren!

You turn on the weather radio. The announcer says that everyone should get to a safe place. At least one tornado has been spotted and is headed into your town. Your mom runs into your room, and you both run into your family's basement to wait—and hope the tornado changes direction. It's your first time experiencing a tornado, and you're scared. You have so many questions. Most importantly, you wonder, "Am I safe?"

WARNING SIRENS

Not every town or city has an outdoor warning siren. However, those that have faced dangerous storms in the past often do. Officials expect people to go inside when they hear the alarm and check news and weather reports. Sirens may only give people a few minutes to act, but that might be enough time to save a life.

It's valuable to know about tornadoes so you can keep yourself out of harm's way if you ever experience one.

WIND POWER

A tornado is a powerful rotating column of wind that reaches down to the ground from a storm cloud. The most deadly tornadoes form from supercells, which are massive thunderstorms.

Supercells occur when a warm **front** and a cold front meet or when a moist, or wet, air mass meets a dry air mass. Warm, moist air rises and **condenses** into rain clouds. Cooler air rushes down, taking the warm air's place. The change in pressure causes wind. When water condenses, it creates energy. This energy further heats up the rising air and strengthens the movement of air both up and down.

NOT SO SURE

Scientists aren't exactly sure why tornadoes form sometimes but not others, even if the conditions seem to be the same. They also don't know why tornadoes end, though they think a mass of cold air cutting off a warm air source is at least part of the reason.

Supercells don't always produce a lot of rain. Sometimes, they make hail.

If there's a strong change in wind speed and direction, the winds may start to spin **horizontally**. And if the spinning winds move over a warm **updraft**, they lift and begin spinning vertically. This spinning cloud mass is called a mesocyclone. There's a 50 percent chance a tornado can form from a mesocyclone.

When a spinning **downdraft** reaches down from the mesocyclone to touch the ground, it's called a tornado. Tornadoes can look like a funnel or like a skinny rope. Some tornadoes have more than one funnel with a common center. Some are almost invisible! A tornado's color comes from the dust and **debris** it picks up.

How a Tornado Begins to Form

mass of air spins horizontally

updraft lifts mass of air, forming a column

column of air gains strength and updraft spins with it

PREDICTABLE UNPREDICTABILITY

Though most tornadoes move from west to east, many don't move in a predictable, or expected, way. Tornadoes can turn or even double back, crossing over the same area again. That's why people should always find shelter when a tornado has been spotted and stay there until they hear it's safe to come out.

A mesocyclone is often several miles wide. Its "wall cloud" is low and easy to spot.

THE EF SCALE

Most tornadoes touch down for just a few minutes, so their strength is hard to measure. In addition, scientific equipment can be torn apart by their strong winds. Since 2007, the National Weather Service (NWS) has been rating tornado strength according to the EF (Enhanced Fujita) Scale. The scale uses the harm a tornado causes to estimate, or guess, its wind speed.

After a storm, NWS officials examine the destruction and match it to the scale's 28 indicators. The officials note not only what structures are damaged, or harmed, but how badly. They use all this information to give the tornado a rating from EF0 to EF5.

WHAT ARE THE INDICATORS?

Twenty-eight indicators are needed in the EF Scale because winds affect different structures in different ways. Structures within the indicators are one- and two-family houses, barns, motels, mobile homes, schools, apartment buildings, trees, flagpoles, and shopping malls. The damage for each is rated from 1 (slight) to 8 (totally destroyed).

The EF Scale is an improved version of the original Fujita Scale. It's thought to have better estimates of wind speed.

THE DAMAGE IT DOES

Tornadoes' incredible wind speeds—sometimes up to 300 miles (483 km) per hour—cause the shocking destruction we often see in the news. Sometimes it's hard to tell what buildings once existed at the scene because they're reduced to sticks of wood.

It doesn't take an especially powerful tornado to rip apart a house. A tornado rated as low as an EF2 can do it. This is what happens: Winds pull up on the roof, while debris breaks windows. The house fills with pressure, further pushing up on the roof as well as on the outside walls. The roof finally lifts off the house, and the walls may come apart, too.

TOO MOBILE

It's common to see pictures of mobile homes destroyed by tornadoes. This is because they're lightweight compared to other homes. A tornado can pick them up and pull them apart. It's advised that those who live in mobile homes should go to a safer place, such as a neighbor's basement, before a tornado.

All this can happen in just a few seconds.

Most tornadoes move about 28 miles (45 km) per hour. They pass through neighborhoods so quickly that parts of a house may be left standing. That's why people can hide safely in basements and inner rooms until they pass.

Besides damage to homes and other buildings, tornadoes impact communities in other ways. Winds blow down tree branches or rip tree roots out of the ground. They take down electrical lines, disconnecting people from power and leaving live wires in streets and yards. The storms from which tornadoes form may bring heavy rains that create more problems, such as flooding.

HELMET HELP?

Flying objects are some of the greatest dangers to people during a tornado. Some officials suggest putting on a bike or football helmet if you're caught outdoors during a tornado. This might prevent a head injury if debris hits your head or if winds pick you up and drop you. However, it's always better to be indoors.

People look through the remains of their home to find belongings after a tornado.

WHAT'S IT LIKE?

What does a tornado feel like? Most people don't know because, smartly, they head into an indoor shelter when they're warned one is coming their way.

However, people have reported what it sounds like passing overhead. Many say a tornado rumbles or roars loudly like a train or a jet engine. Others say it makes a whooshing sound like a waterfall. They hear other noises caused by the high winds, such as wires snapping, trees cracking, and glass and wood cracking. They say the suddenly dropping air pressure tornadoes cause makes their ears "pop."

EYE WITNESSES

Amazingly, a few people have survived being in the eye, or center, of a tornado. Two farmers reported getting caught outside accidentally. Each said that everything was calm in the eye. The inner cloud walls were smooth, and lightning zigzagged from side to side. One man described seeing little tornadoes form from the big one. Incredibly, neither was hurt by their experience.

You don't want to be outdoors when tornado winds are ripping apart your neighborhood.

PREPARE LIKE A PRO

Talk with your family about **emergency** plans in the event of a tornado. Once you hear a tornado warning, you can set your plan into action. Your family should have a place to wait for the tornado to pass, preferably underground, such as a basement or storm cellar, or an inside room that doesn't have a window.

Make sure you have supplies in case you need to stay indoors for a while. These should include a first-aid kit, flashlight, food that won't spoil, water, and a battery-powered radio. It's also smart to have a fully charged cell phone and **flares** to contact or signal others.

If a tornado watch turns into a tornado warning, that means a tornado has touched down. Head directly to the nearest safe shelter, wherever you are. Some communities have public shelters.

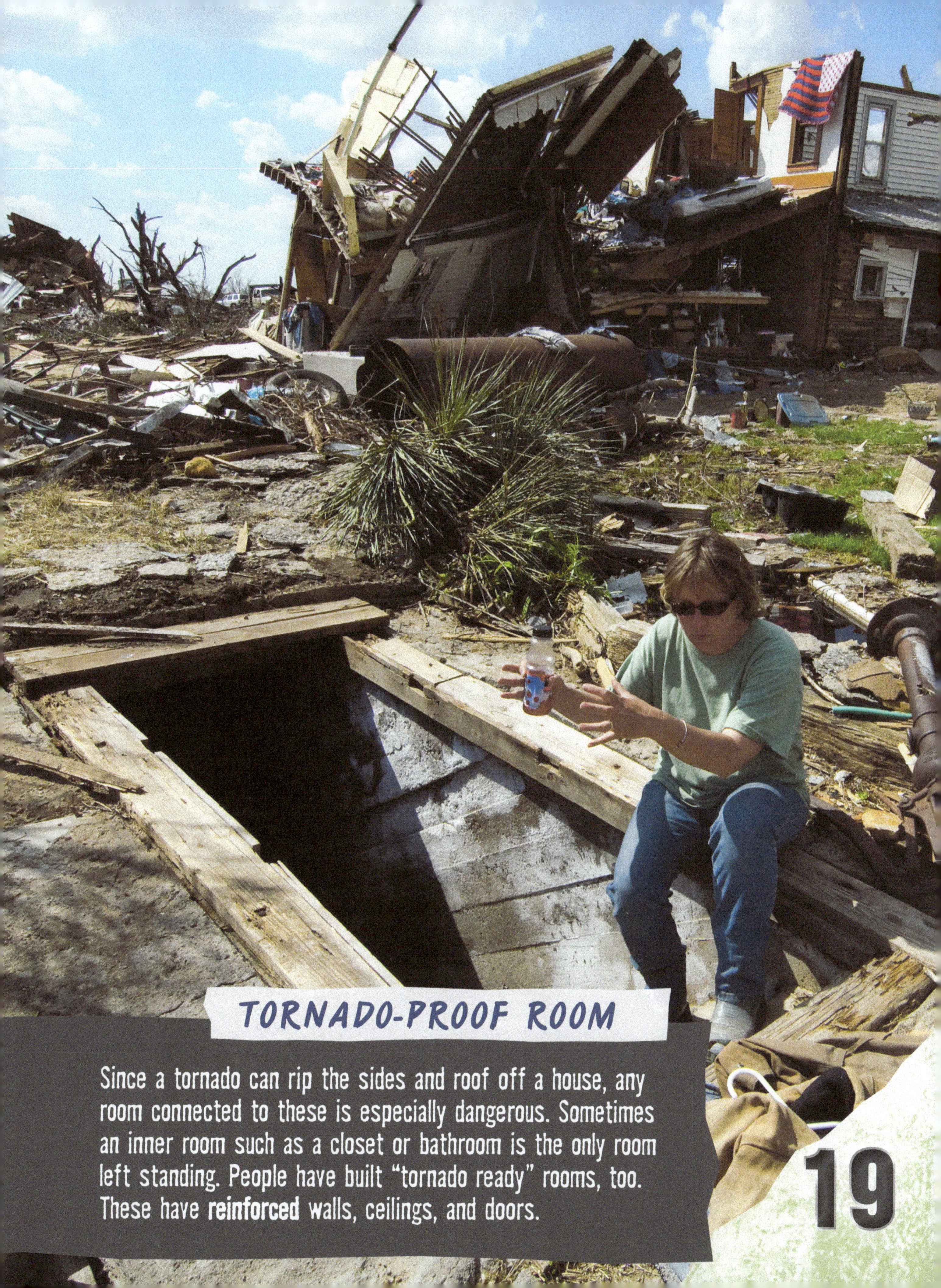

TORNADO-PROOF ROOM

Since a tornado can rip the sides and roof off a house, any room connected to these is especially dangerous. Sometimes an inner room such as a closet or bathroom is the only room left standing. People have built "tornado ready" rooms, too. These have **reinforced** walls, ceilings, and doors.

Since tornadoes can appear so quickly, sometimes people are caught near one while on the road. Tornadoes can travel as quickly as cars and don't have to follow the road, so it's best not to try to outrace one. A car or truck may be picked up and pushed over by winds, so leave the car if possible. Look for a nearby fast-food restaurant or a bank. Each usually has an inner room that would be safe to hide in.

Sometimes drivers try to find shelter under an overpass. However, this is actually more dangerous than staying on the open road. Wind speeds can increase under an overpass when a tornado passes.

GET DOWN!

If no shelter is nearby while you're in a car when a tornado approaches, most authorities advise getting out of the car or truck and lying in a ditch with your head covered until it's safe. It doesn't offer a lot of protection, but this may save your life if debris is flying overhead.

Outdriving a tornado isn't always possible. You need an emergency plan when in the car, too.

TERRIFYING TORNADOES

The United States averages more than 1,000 tornadoes a year, more than any other nation. Canada has the second-highest number of tornadoes with about 100. Most of these tornadoes are weak and short-lived. However, some tornadoes are so deadly and destructive that they've changed landscapes—and lives—forever.

One of the worst tornadoes in recent years struck Missouri, especially the town of Joplin, on May 22, 2011. Its winds measured more than 200 miles (322 km) per hour. The EF5 tornado traveled about 22 miles (35 km) over 38 minutes, destroying more than 7,000 homes, killing 158 people, and injuring more than 1,000.

The cost of rebuilding Joplin and a neighboring town after the tornado has topped more than $1 billion so far.

HOW STRONG IS AN EF5?

The Joplin tornado showed the strength of an EF5. Wood-framed homes were totally destroyed, while steel-reinforced concrete structures were ripped from the ground. A bank was wiped out—leaving just a concrete safe. The tornado grew to be about 1 mile (1.6 km) wide, so the damage was widespread.

Many historians think the worst tornado in US history was the Tri-State Tornado of 1925. On March 18, it passed through three states: Missouri, Illinois, and Indiana, a distance of 219 miles (352 km). It spent about 3 hours on the ground and traveled as fast as 70 miles (113 km) per hour at times. In all, 695 people were killed, more than 500 of those in southern Illinois.

The record-breaking tornado was the longest in US history. It also killed the most people and resulted in the most injuries—more than 2,000.

DEADLIEST IN THE WORLD

The deadliest tornado in the world occurred in Bangladesh in 1989. For the 10 miles (16 km) it was on the ground, it destroyed every structure it touched. About 1,300 people died, 12,000 were injured, and another 80,000 were left homeless. Poor building construction and no warning system were given as reasons for the terrible damage.

Unaware of the storm above, men working deep in an underground mine in Illinois came up to find their town destroyed after the Tri-State Tornado.

FRUSTRATING FORECASTS

A weather scientist once called tornadoes "the hardest forecasting problem of all." **Meteorologists** can figure out when the conditions are right for severe thunderstorms, which may or may not create tornadoes. However, they often can't put out a warning until just minutes before a tornado forms—if they have time to put out a warning at all. Conditions in the atmosphere change quickly, making their job very challenging.

Forecasting is getting better, though. **Radar** systems and computer models are helping meteorologists track air rotation and better **predict** where tornadoes may touch down. Tornado warning time has increased from an average of 5 minutes in the 1980s to about 13 minutes today.

TORNADO ALLEY

Tornado Alley is the nickname given to an area of the United States that experiences many tornadoes each year. According to some, it stretches from Texas north to South Dakota and from Colorado east to Missouri. Florida and other Gulf Coast states face many tornadoes, too. However, every US state has reported tornadoes.

The National Weather Service is usually the agency that issues tornado watches and warnings. They often work together with the National Severe Storms Laboratory.

ARE YOU READY?

Now that you've read a lot about tornadoes, you know there's a lot we don't know about them. Most importantly, we don't know exactly when they'll strike. Until meteorologists and other scientists figure that out, the best thing you can do is be prepared to protect yourself should you hear a tornado warning.

Talk with your family and friends about your emergency plans. Remember, if you're lucky enough to get a warning, you'll probably only have a few minutes to act. Tornadoes are some of the most dangerous weather events you could ever experience. So, keep your eye on the sky and as far away from a tornado as possible!

CHASERS AND SPOTTERS

There are people who actually want to be near tornadoes. They're called tornado chasers. Most are scientists who race to collect information about a tornado as it's happening to learn more about them. Spotters are ordinary people who report the weather where they live to the National Weather Service. Their job is extremely important, too. They may be the first to spot a tornado.

TORNADOES: MYTHS AND FACTS

MYTH	FACT
Opening windows can keep a house from being destroyed.	A tornado can destroy a house with open windows.
Tornadoes don't hit cities.	Tornadoes can form anywhere.
Tornadoes don't cross water.	Tornadoes can cross and even form over water.
You can hide from a tornado in the southwest corner of a building.	Tornadoes may hit any corner of a building.
Tornadoes don't strike the same place twice.	Tornadoes can form anywhere and anytime.
The size and shape of a tornado tells you how strong it is.	Tornado strength can only be measured by the damage it does.

Even tornado chasers in special vehicles have been killed in tornadoes. This job may seem exciting, but it's very dangerous, too.

GLOSSARY

condense: to lose heat and change from a gas into a liquid

debris: the remains of something that has been broken

downdraft: a downward flow of air

emergency: an unexpected situation that needs quick action

flare: a tool used to produce light as a signal calling for help

front: the border between two masses of air

horizontally: in a manner level with the line that seems to form where the earth meets the sky

meteorologist: one who studies Earth's atmosphere, especially to forecast weather

predict: to guess what will happen in the future based on facts or knowledge

radar: a machine that uses radio waves to locate and identify objects

reinforced: strengthened with additional material such as metal wire or rods

updraft: an upward flow of air

FOR MORE INFORMATION

BOOKS

Adamson, Heather. *Surviving a Tornado.* Mankato, MN: Amicus Readers, 2012.

Hubbard, Ben. *Tornado: Perspectives on Tornado Disasters.* Chicago, IL: Capstone Heinemann Library, 2015.

Rudolph, Jessica. *Tornado.* New York, NY: Bearport Publishing, 2014.

WEBSITES

Severe Weather 101: Tornadoes
www.nssl.noaa.gov/education/svrwx101/tornadoes/
Read more about tornadoes on this National Severe Storms Laboratory site.

Tornadoes
www.weatherwizkids.com/weather-tornado.htm
Find pictures, diagrams, and more on this tornado website.

Publisher's note to educators and parents: Our editors have carefully reviewed these websites to ensure that they are suitable for students. Many websites change frequently, however, and we cannot guarantee that a site's future contents will continue to meet our high standards of quality and educational value. Be advised that students should be closely supervised whenever they access the Internet.

INDEX